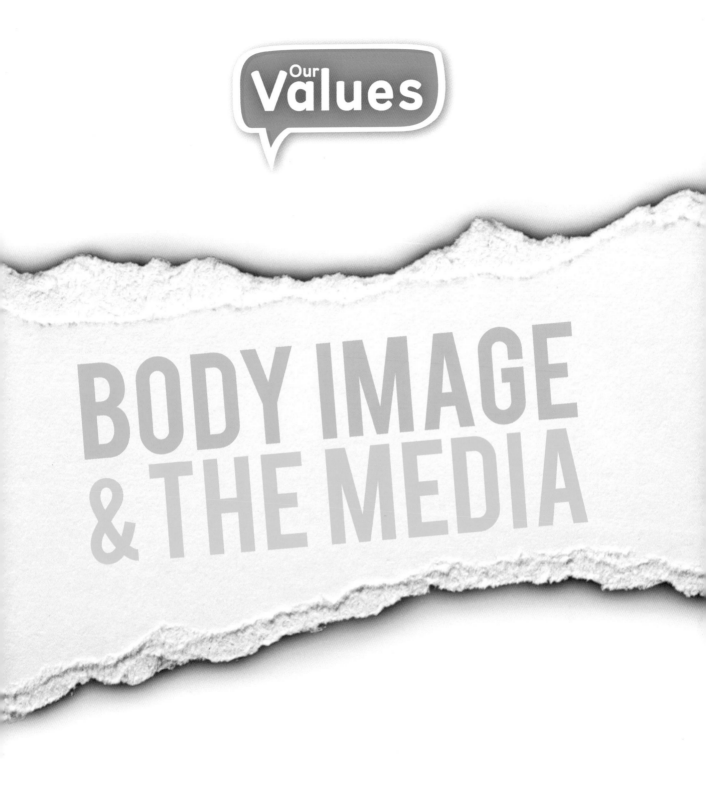

Our Values

BODY IMAGE & THE MEDIA

by

Grace Jones

CRABTREE
PUBLISHING COMPANY
WWW.CRABTREEBOOKS.COM

Published in Canada
Crabtree Publishing
616 Welland Avenue
St. Catharines, ON
L2M 5V6

Published in the United States
Crabtree Publishing
PMB 59051
350 Fifth Ave, 59th Floor
New York, NY 10118

Published in 2019 by Crabtree Publishing Company

First Published by Book Life in 2018
Copyright © 2018 Book Life

Author: Grace Jones

Editors: Holly Duhig, Janine Deschenes

Design: Daniel Scase

Proofreader: Ellen Rodger

Production coordinator and
  prepress technician (interior): Margaret Amy Salter

Prepress technician (covers): Ken Wright

Print coordinator: Katharine Berti

All facts, statistics, web addresses and URLs in this book were verified as valid and accurate at time of writing.
No responsibility for any changes to external websites or references can be accepted by either the author or publisher.

Printed in the U.S.A./082018/CG20180601

Photographs

Front Cover – Natee K Jindakum, easy camera.
2 – Patrick Foto. 4 – MJTH. 5 – Rawpixel.com, Syda Productions.
6 – By Phovoir. 7 – Rawpixel.com. 8 – ASDF_MEDIA, tommaso79.
9 – Stuart Miles. 10 – Christian Bertrand. 11 – luanateutzi.
12 – Andrey_Popov. 13 – Rawpixel.com. 14 – Lipik Stock Media.
15 – CREATISTA. 16 – Syda Productions. 17 – FrameStockFootages, CBS Radio. 18 – By FashionStock.com, karelnoppe. 19 – staras, Daniel M Ernst. 20 – Valery Sidelnykov. 21 – Sandra van der Steen.
22 – oliveromg. 23 – Christos Georghiou. 24 – Jaren Jai Wicklund.
25 – Syda Productions, Rawpixel.com.
26 – SteveSimonsPhotography. 27 – Syda Productions. 28 – Paolo Bona. 29 – Anna Om. 30 – Dragon Images.

Library and Archives Canada Cataloguing in Publication

Jones, Grace, 1990-, author
        Body image and the media / Grace Jones.

(Our values)
Includes index.
Issued in print and electronic formats.
ISBN 978-0-7787-5189-2 (hardcover).--
ISBN 978-0-7787-5200-4 (softcover).--
ISBN 978-1-4271-2139-4 (HTML)

        1. Body image--Juvenile literature. 2. Body image--Social aspects--Juvenile literature. 3. Mass media--Juvenile literature. 4. Mass media--Social aspects--Juvenile literature. 5. Mass media--Psychological aspects--Juvenile literature. 6. Mass media--Influence--Juvenile literature. I. Title.

BF697.5.B63J65 2018   j306.4'613   C2018-902413-5
                                                 C2018-902414-3

Library of Congress Cataloging-in-Publication Data

CIP available at the Library of Congress

CONTENTS

Words that are **boldfaced** can be found in the glossary on page 31.

WHAT IS BODY IMAGE?

Body image is a phrase you have probably heard at home, at school, or in the media. Everyone has a body image. But what does this phrase actually mean? Body image is the way you see your physical appearance.

It is your thoughts, attitudes, and **perceptions** about your body. Body image is a broad phrase that can encompass, or include, a lot of different thoughts, beliefs, feelings, and experiences.

HOW DO YOU FEEL ABOUT YOUR APPEARANCE WHEN YOU LOOK IN THE MIRROR?

The emotional feelings and beliefs you have about your body and other aspects of your appearance, such as your facial features, are part of your body image. It includes how you feel about your body's capabilities, and how you think others view your appearance.

Your body image includes the way you physically feel in your body as you experience the world. Are you comfortable in your body as you move around? How does your body feel when you participate in an activity or show your strength?

NEGATIVE BODY IMAGE

Someone who has a negative or unhealthy body image is unhappy with their appearance. They may feel that their body, facial features, or other parts of their appearance are unattractive and want to change them. Usually, this mindset is accompanied by feelings of having less **value**, or worth, as a person. A negative body image often means that a person negatively compares themselves to others and have difficulty recognizing the good things about their bodies. It also often means that a person has a **distorted** view of how they look.

A PERSON WHO HAS A POSITIVE BODY IMAGE DOES NOT FEEL LIKE THEY NEED TO CHANGE HOW THEY LOOK.

POSITIVE BODY IMAGE

Having a positive or healthy body image means that you like the way you look and are comfortable in your body. It means that you recognize and accept your natural body shape, and you have an accurate perception of your appearance—which means that you see your body and other features the way they really are. Body positivity also means that you understand that a person's value comes from much more than their appearance.

WHAT IS SELF-ESTEEM?

Your body image is closely related to your self-esteem. This is the opinion that you have about yourself, or how much you like who you are. Self-esteem affects many parts of your life. It affects how you see your value or **self-worth**, which usually influences how you take care of yourself physically and emotionally. A person who has high self-esteem, or likes themselves inside and out, is likely to have a positive body image, too. It also works the other way. Liking your body or the way you look can be one part of having positive self-esteem.

SELF-CARE

A person who has high self-esteem thinks positively about themselves and believes that they are valuable and important as a person. How you view your self-worth is related to how you take care of yourself. Self-care can mean that you stay healthy by eating, sleeping, and exercising. It can mean that you take care of your **mental health** by acknowledging your emotions, accepting your mistakes, and celebrating your accomplishments. Self-care also means that you respect yourself. Having self-respect means that you feel you deserve to be treated well by yourself and others. It also means you keep yourself safe and act in a way that you feel is moral, or right.

SELF-CONFIDENCE

Self-confidence describes feelings of positivity about your abilities and your **qualities**. High self-confidence is usually associated with high self-esteem, high feelings of self-worth, and a positive body image. Having self-confidence can help you develop good friendships, try new things, and help you feel good about the way you look. Knowing what makes you happy and how to reach your goals can help you feel strong and in control of your life.

CONFIDENCE DOESN'T ALWAYS COME NATURALLY, BUT IT CAN BE PRACTICED AND IMPROVED.

There are many things that can affect our self-esteem in a negative way. Comparing ourselves to others is one common practice that can harm how we feel about ourselves. Pictures on social media or other online sites often show others at their best. Celebrities are professionally made-up and dressed to impress. Our peers often post only their most flattering photos. Recognizing that these photos aren't always reflections of reality can help improve how we feel about ourselves. Other times, negative comments on our appearance from others can affect our self-esteem. No matter the reason for their comments, it is important to remember that self-esteem and feelings of worth come from within—not from bullies' opinions.

WHAT IS THE MEDIA?

The word "media" refers to any form of **mass communication** that information is delivered through. This can include newspapers, radios, advertisements, televisions, magazines, the Internet, and social media. Every day, people hear or see many different types of media. The messages that are communicated in the media affect the way we see ourselves and the world around us.

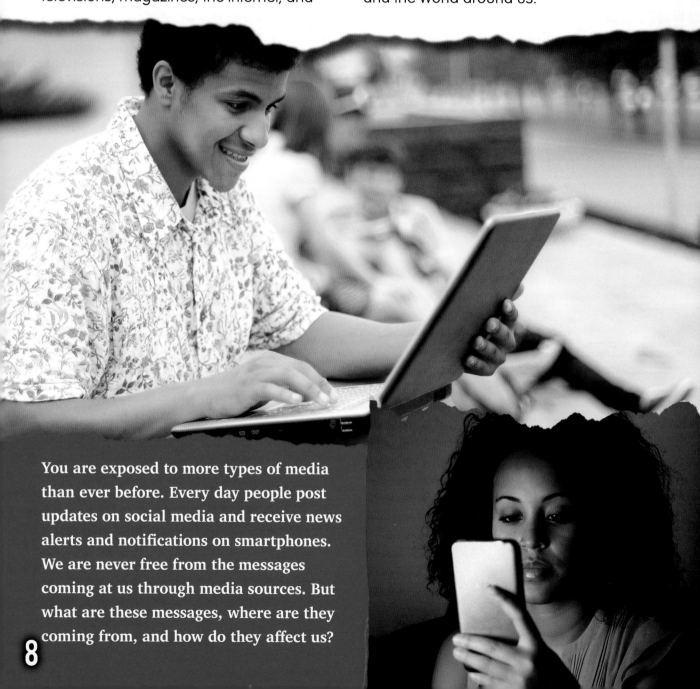

You are exposed to more types of media than ever before. Every day people post updates on social media and receive news alerts and notifications on smartphones. We are never free from the messages coming at us through media sources. But what are these messages, where are they coming from, and how do they affect us?

Through media channels, the opinions of one person, company, or organization are heard by hundreds, thousands, or millions of other people. These messages are sometimes about body image. Think about the different messages you have heard about body image. Where did they come from? A fitness model on Instagram might post images of his or her body to gain followers or sell fitness products. A cosmetics company might post images of beautiful women to sell some eyeliner. Shows on TV might feature popular, happy characters who don't look like you. Each of these messages imply that we need to look a certain way.

Media can be a good thing because it can allow people to keep up-to-date with what is going on in the world. Social media allows us to connect with other people—even with celebrities and people we admire. But sometimes, the messages we receive can be upsetting or false.

In advertisements, we see photoshopped models. On social media, we see pictures of seemingly "perfect" celebrities and even strangers. All of the messages we receive have an effect on our self-esteem, body image, and feelings of self-worth.

BODY IMAGE AND THE MEDIA

The growth of different types of media, especially social media, has changed the way that we can access and view information. Because of this, its influence and impact has grown too. Think about the people you see in the media you access each day. They might be actors in a TV show or movie, peers and influencers on social media, hosts of talk shows and news broadcasts, and actors or models featured in advertisements. What do they look like? Can you identify any similarities between the looks of the majority of people featured in the media?

Examine how the actors who play an aspiring actress (center) and physicists are presented in this image of the TV show *The Big Bang Theory*. What messages are being sent about how certain types of people look?

The people we see featured in the media every day influence what we perceive to be **conventionally attractive**. Are most men in leading roles tall, fit, and masculine? What about leading women? Do they have slim body types, wear fashionable clothing, and have flawless skin?

What kinds of roles are played by men and women who do not look this way? Do men and women who look a certain way get the most Instagram likes or YouTube views? The more we see certain types of people featured and celebrated in the media we are exposed to, the more we believe that everyone should look like them.

UNREALISTIC EXPECTATIONS

Often, the images we see in the media have been **edited** or "airbrushed." Airbrushing describes changing a photo from the original to make the subject look more attractive. It can be used to make the ocean look more blue in a tourism advertisement. It can also make a model look more slim or more muscular, remove **blemishes** and imperfections, and even alter facial features to appear more conventionally attractive. When used in this way, airbrushing and photo editing can cause people to have unrealistic expectations of how they should look. When we compare ourselves to photos that are not true representations of people's looks, it is difficult to remember that real bodies—with imperfections and different shapes—should be celebrated.

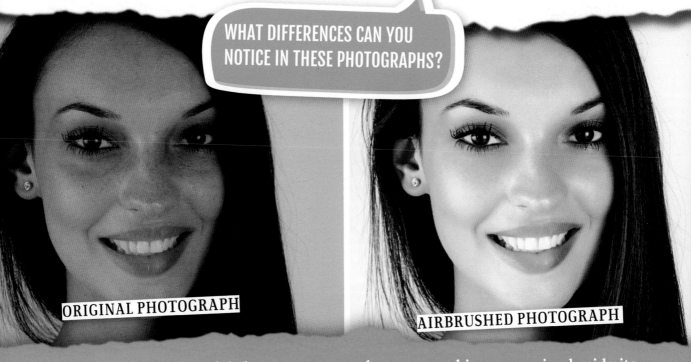

WHAT DIFFERENCES CAN YOU NOTICE IN THESE PHOTOGRAPHS?

ORIGINAL PHOTOGRAPH

AIRBRUSHED PHOTOGRAPH

Some celebrities and models have spoken out against magazines and advertisements that edit photos of them. Actor Kate Winslet used social media to tell her followers that one magazine had airbrushed her legs to make them appear more thin. American actor and singer Zendaya posted an edited photo that appeared in a magazine beside its original. In the edited version, Zendaya's already-slim body had been altered so that it was unrealistically small. She influenced the magazine to fix the issue and pointed out how the original photo showed a normal body shape.

SOCIAL MEDIA

Social media is one of the most used forms of media. On social media, users can interact with their friends, families, celebrities, and even complete strangers. Many social media sites focus on image sharing. Because of this, social media can have a big impact on people's own body image. Research shows a strong link between a person's body image, their self-esteem, and their social-media usage. The prevalence of social media means that people are constantly exposed to **idealized** images of their peers and of celebrities. Sites that allow people to "like" and comment on photos means that people receive constant feedback on their looks.

OVER 2.5 BILLION PEOPLE USE SOCIAL MEDIA SITES AND THIS NUMBER IS GROWING EVERY SINGLE YEAR.

SOCIAL MEDIA: THE FACTS

- Facebook: 1,871 million users
- Whatsapp: 1,000 million users
- Instagram: 600 million users
- Twitter: 317 million users
- Snapchat: 300 million users

Many social media sites such as Facebook, Instagram and Snapchat allow people to share images of themselves wherever and whenever they want to. Research has shown that the more that users **engage** with the social media site that they are using—for example by sharing posts and commenting on other people's—the more likely they are to link their self-worth to their appearance. Social media users often connect how they look in a photo to the number of likes or positive comments they get. Unfortunately, this means that social media can negatively affect the self-esteem of users.

"Likes" and comments on social media often teach users that certain types of bodies are admired and celebrated. Some users feel pressured to make sure their picture gets a high number of "likes." Research has shown that they connect the feedback they receive on their photo with their appearance and their self-worth. It's difficult to avoid comparing oneself with users on social media who get thousands of likes and comments on their posts. But our self-worth is not tied up in how our photos look and the number of likes we get.

It's important to remember that most people put only their best face forward on social media. They post photos that may not be accurate representations of their lives. Some social media platforms, such as Instagram and Snapchat, allow users to edit their photos before posting them. There are also apps that can be used to photoshop photos before posting them to social media. This means that a lot of pictures shared on social media are unrealistic representations of what people actually look like.

MEDIA POSITIVITY

Media messages can have a negative impact on creating and maintaining a positive body image and positive self-esteem. However, recent trends have shown how the media can also be a positive influence on the way we see our bodies and ourselves! In 2004, the Dove Campaign for Real Beauty was launched.

Its goal is to represent all body types in Dove advertisements, showing that all types of appearances should be equally celebrated and encouraging all people to be confident in their bodies. Television shows, movies, and documentaries are tackling topics about body image and showing viewers that it's okay to be yourself.

Despite the tendency for social media users to compare themselves with others, and the prevalence of highly-edited photos that celebrate certain body types, social media can also have a positive impact on our body image and self-esteem. There are movements on social media that call out how photos are unrealistic representations of real life. Some social media users post "before" and "after" photos that show how photos are edited and posed to look a certain way. Other social media accounts promote body positivity, mental wellness, and a healthy lifestyle. People can connect with one another to offer support and tips. We can benefit from social media by seeking out and creating these kinds of messages.

It can be difficult to foster a positive body image despite all of the media influences we are exposed to. Here are some tips to remember when viewing media:

- Ignore those who think that the "ideal" body exists, it doesn't. Airbrushing and photo editing creates unrealistic expectations for body image. This doesn't exist in professional photos only. Airbrushing can be found in photos on social media, too.
- Recognize when the media is sending messages about appearance that are meant to sell a product. Many products rely on making **consumers** feel like their natural appearance is not enough.
- Avoid types of media that focus on changing your appearance. Seek out media that promotes a postive body image and a positive lifestyle.
- Look out for media that promotes harmful gender stereotypes. Men do not have to be physically strong to be attractive. Women are valued for more than their **sex appeal**. All people deserve love and affection.
- Remember there is no such thing as "normal." Each person is **unique** and original—that's what makes us human.

IF WE ARE TAUGHT TO VALUE AND LOVE OURSELVES NO MATTER WHAT, THEN MESSAGES IN THE MEDIA ARE MUCH LESS LIKELY TO HAVE A NEGATIVE EFFECT ON THE WAY THAT WE SEE OURSELVES.

DIVERSITY AND REPRESENTATION

The images we see in the media have a profound effect on the way we see ourselves. How the media represents— or does not represent—different kinds of people influences our thoughts about them and ourselves. To represent means to stand for or symbolize. When you read or view media, do you feel that you are represented? Do you see people who look like you, who think like you, or who lead similar lives?

GENDER, ETHNICITY, AGE, BODY SHAPE, AND HEIGHT ARE ALL WAYS WE ARE DIVERSE.

RESEARCH HAS SHOWN THAT THE MORE YOU ARE EXPOSED TO DIVERSITY IN THE MEDIA, THE MORE LIKELY YOU ARE TO HAVE BODY CONFIDENCE.

Often, the media does not accurately represent the diverse world that we live in. The people around us each day have different cultures, ethnicities, genders, ages, beliefs, interests, and body types. But often, we see the same types of people represented in media. Seeing the same types of people represented can lead us to believe that everyone should look, think, and act in that way. When we compare ourselves to the people we see in the media, we may feel that the ways we are different from them are wrong. This can have a big effect on our self-esteem and body image.

The people and **corporations** who create the media represent people in specific ways to get a specific reaction from the audience. A company selling beauty products will show a conventionally attractive person using that product—with the goal of making consumers feel that they need the product and are not attractive enough on their own. Producers of news organizations might sell more newspapers or gain more TV viewers by using negative language to describe **minority** populations. Directors of movies and TV shows might **whitewash** roles in order to use well-known white actors who will draw a large audience. In 2016, a campaign to make the film industry more inclusive of people of different ethnicities began. It started because of the lack of diversity in the nominees for the famous Academy Awards, also known as the Oscars. Campaigns like these aim to improve diversity in media representation. They also combat **misrepresentation**.

IN 1940, HATTIE MCDANIEL BECAME THE FIRST BLACK ACTOR TO WIN AN OCSAR. SHE WON BEST SUPPORTING ACTRESS FOR HER ROLE IN *GONE WITH THE WIND.*

BODY IMAGE AND ABILITY

If you don't see yourself or people like you in the media you watch and read, it can make you feel like your body is different or not accepted. Films, TV shows, and the fashion industry tend to represent only a certain type of body; most often tall, thin, **able-bodied** people. This can cause people who don't look like this to have negative body images. People who have disabilities are often not represented in the media and this can affect body image. A disability is a condition that impairs a person's physical or mental abilities. When people who have disabilities are featured, they do not usually have leading roles or are not featured as an example of beauty.

When someone who has an intellectual disability is portrayed in the media, are they usually shown as capable of doing normal activities, such as working?

Many people are fighting back against this lack of representation. Models with all kinds of physical disabilities are modelling clothes on the catwalk at big fashion events such as London fashion week. In some forms of media, such as the TV show *This is Us*, mental illness and ability is being addressed in a way that reduces its stigma. As people with all abilities are represented in media, we can start to erase negative beliefs about people based on their ability.

CAN WE TRUST WHAT WE SEE?

Representation of different models who have different heights and body shapes in the media has grown. Some companies, such as the clothing company Aerie, runs ads showing a range of body types. This kind of representation has challenged the idea that there is an "ideal" height or size.

> IT IS IMPORTANT TO REMEMBER THAT THE WAY PEOPLE ARE REPRESENTED THROUGH THE MEDIA MIGHT NOT ACCURATELY REPRESENT REAL LIFE.

We know that the media often airbrushes images of celebrities in magazines and newspapers to change their appearances, but there are many more ways in which the media can give us false representations of reality. For example, people on television often go through many changes to their appearances before they are considered "TV ready." They may have a team of hairdressers, **stylists** to dress them, and makeup artists to change their appearances. All these things mean that what we see on TV is not a "natural" representation of what people really look like.

GENDER AND BODY IMAGE

We get many of our perceptions and beliefs from the media. We know that the way the media represents people can influence the way we think about them. Representation can sometimes lead to stereotypes. Stereotypes are oversimplified ideas about a person or group of people. Common stereotypes often represented in media are traditional gender roles. From a young age, messages and images in the media teach us that boys and girls act in certain ways, have certain interests, and should look a certain way.

How does this image send a message about how men and women should spend their time?

Gender stereotypes affect our body image in many ways. Our body image has a lot to do with how we dress. When we dress in the clothes we like to wear, we feel confident and good about ourselves. But in the media, girls and women often dress in a different way than boys and men. Clothing companies market certain clothing for certain genders. But clothing is not gender-specific. Clothes are for everyone, and it is okay to have a different style from what you see in the media.

Sex refers to the biological differences between the bodies of males and females. On the other hand, gender has more to do with your **identity**, or how you see yourself. Most people are not completely masculine or completely feminine. For people who are transgender, their sex does not match their gender. How you present, or show, your gender to the world is a reflection of your identity. It is okay if how you choose to present yourself does not match traditional gender roles that are usually the most commonly represented in the media.

GENDER IS ONE MORE WAY THAT WE ARE DIVERSE FROM ONE ANOTHER—AND IT IS NOT ALWAYS REPRESENTED WELL IN THE MEDIA.

It can be extremely challenging for a person to have a positive body image if they feel that they do not fit in with the traditional roles represented in the media. It becomes even more challenging when non-traditional genders are misrepresented or stereotyped in the media. A woman who has a masculine appearance is not always a tough person. A man who has a feminine appearance is not always weak. A person's appearance does not relate to their sexual preference, or the gender they are attracted to. Media that says or implies otherwise may be reinforcing stereotypes.

21

EXERCISE AND BODY IMAGE

Exercise is good for your physical health and your mental health too. When we exercise, chemicals called **endorphins** are released in our brains. They make us feel happy and good about ourselves. Exercise also burns body fat, so many people exercise to maintain a healthy body weight.

After you take part in a sport or activity it is important to replace the energy you have used up with a healthy snack.

Regular exercise can also help you to develop good self-esteem. This is partly because exercise is about reaching goals. Goals might include such things as "I want to win the soccer championship with my team," "I want to beat my personal best swimming time," or "I want to be able to run five miles." Reaching your goals can make you feel good about yourself. Some people may also follow a healthy, balanced diet. Following a healthy diet can give you more energy and even help to change your mood, which can boost self-esteem.

Exercise can also, unfortunately, be taken too far. Some people see exercise as a way to change their bodies when they have an unhealthy body image. It is possible to become addicted to or obsessed with exercise for the wrong reasons, and lose too much body fat. Just as having too much body fat can be unhealthy, so can having too little.

People who play sports competitively are often encouraged to keep their bodies in peak condition with strict exercise and diets—which can also lead to a negative body image. In extreme cases, **eating disorders** can result from having an unhealthy relationship between body image and exercise.

A negative body image and pressure to be thin means that sometimes, exercise results in people losing too much weight. But exercise can also be taken too far by people who want to gain muscle. In the media, men often have strong bodies with big muscles. From action and superhero movies to advertisements,

men are pressured to also build a muscular physique. This can cause men to exercise to change their bodies to reflect that body type. However, this is an unrealistic representation of how men should look. As long as your body is healthy, there is no need to over-exercise.

TAKING CARE OF YOUR SELF-ESTEEM

We already know that the media can strongly influence how we feel about ourselves, but the growth of social media sites and users can mean that sometimes it is hard for us to avoid or cope with this influence. Below are some top tips and ways that can help you to cope with pressure.

The media is a huge influence in our lives. Social media is growing every day. We spend a large portion of our days consuming different kinds of media. This means that sometimes it is hard for us to avoid or cope with the negative messages that media can send about body image.

Sometimes the negative messages can feel overwhelming or inescapable, and influence our self-esteem. But there are some strategies that can help. The next page gives tips that can help you to cope with media pressure.

COPING WITH MEDIA PRESSURE

Acccept yourself the way that you are. Everyone has imperfections. We are all unique and original and that's what makes us human.

Focus on the good things about your body. Try to recognize all of the things your body can do and all of the things you like about it.

Compliment yourself and others. Focus on the positive things about yourself and other people. Learn to accept compliments, too. You are deserving of them.

Remember that everyone is valuable and important. How you look does not decide how much you are worth. It's what's on the inside that really matters.

Treat others how you'd like to be treated. Sometimes people with low self-esteem criticize the way that others look because they are feeling bad about themselves. This is not OK.

Focus on yourself. Your body is important, but so is your brain. Looking after your mental health is important too. Doing the things that make you happy or learning a new skill can help build your confidence.

Try to avoid engaging with negative forms of media. Sometimes this is not always possible, but try not to read, watch, or listen to types of media that will negatively affect your self-esteem. Seek out pages and users that promote positive body image and self-esteem.

Talk to someone. If low self-esteem or body image problems are becoming too much for you to cope with by yourself, then it can help to talk to a parent, teacher, or a trusted adult about how you feel.

SELF-EXPRESSION AND APPEARANCE

One strategy that can help improve your body image and your self-esteem is to express your interests and beliefs through your appearance. This way, your appearance can be a positive outlet for you to express yourself! Some people like to try different things with their appearance, such as developing a personal clothing style, wearing makeup, or dying their hair. Dressing in clothing that makes us feel comfortable can help us feel good about our bodies. Expressing ourselves through our appearance can also help us feel more confident and self assured.

By dying their hair and wearing dark clothes these people are expressing their love of this gothic style.

Developing a personal style can be fun and can help you make friends who share a similar style. It's important to remember that sometimes, changing our appearance means that we need to take **responsibility** for the choices we make. While some changes we make to our bodies, such as styling our hair, are **temporary**, other changes, such as getting a tattoo or a piercing, are more **permanent**.

MAKEUP

One way in which people temporarily change their appearance is with makeup. Many people find makeup a fun and creative way of expressing themselves. Makeup is also a skill that people feel proud to learn! Some people upload videos on websites such as YouTube to show off their makeup skills in makeup tutorials. This can be a positive outlet for people to feel proud of their appearance!

Your appearance can be one way you can express yourself and show body positivity. However, if you feel pressure to change your appearance to "fit in," or you don't feel like a worthwhile person unless you change the way you look, this is a sign of a negative body image. Make sure you are comfortable with how you present yourself to the world, and don't give in to pressure to look a certain way. For example, makeup can be a way for people to express themselves through their appearance. But, some people feel pressure to wear makeup to cover any imperfections on their face. It is very easy to watch makeup tutorial videos on YouTube and compare yourself to the people who make the videos. It is important to remember that the people in these videos don't look like this naturally or even all the time. Lighting, filters, and editing can all make a person on film look very different in real life.

27

POSITIVE SELF-ESTEEM STRATEGIES

There are many ways you can develop a positive body image and healthy self-esteem. Knowing what makes you happy and doing more of it is a good way of building self-esteem. Taking part in sports and activities such as music, games, yoga, rugby, and football can help keep you mentally and physically healthy, and boost your self-esteem. Make a list of at least three activities that make you happy. How do you feel when you are participating in these activities? Focusing on the skills you have learned and the capabilities of your body to participate in these activities can help improve your body image!

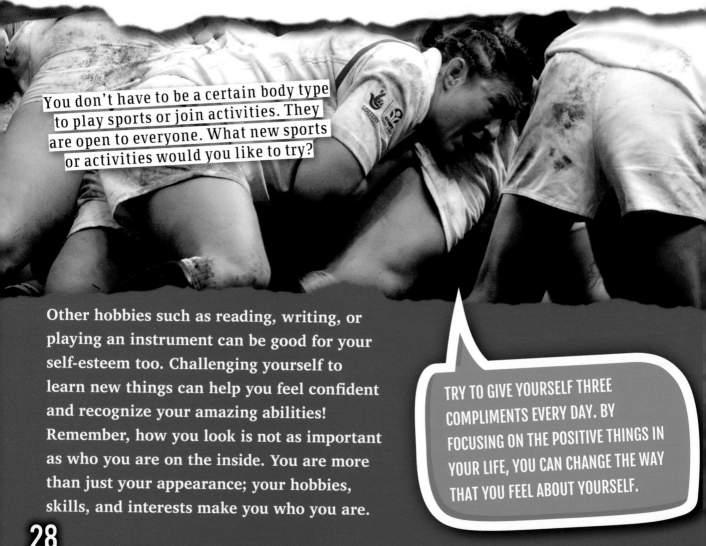

You don't have to be a certain body type to play sports or join activities. They are open to everyone. What new sports or activities would you like to try?

Other hobbies such as reading, writing, or playing an instrument can be good for your self-esteem too. Challenging yourself to learn new things can help you feel confident and recognize your amazing abilities! Remember, how you look is not as important as who you are on the inside. You are more than just your appearance; your hobbies, skills, and interests make you who you are.

TRY TO GIVE YOURSELF THREE COMPLIMENTS EVERY DAY. BY FOCUSING ON THE POSITIVE THINGS IN YOUR LIFE, YOU CAN CHANGE THE WAY THAT YOU FEEL ABOUT YOURSELF.

BODY POSITIVITY

Being body positive is all about accepting your body the way it is. Here are some tips on body positivity!

1. Don't avoid the mirror! When you look in the mirror, think of something you like about yourself.
2. Be positive about other people's appearances. When you notice things that you like about other people's looks, you can start to change the way you think about your own body. Magazines and newspapers will often be critical about a celebrity's appearance to sell more copies. You might hear someone criticize another person's appearance to make themselves feel better. This teaches us to judge others for the way they look. The more we change these negative comments to positive ones, the better we will feel about ourselves.
3. Notice and appreciate all of the amazing things your body can do. It carries you around each day, allows you to show off your sports, music, or speaking skills, and enables you to connect with others.

YOU CAN BE A POSITIVE INFLUENCE ON SOMEONE ELSE'S BODY IMAGE AND SELF-ESTEEM. SPREAD POSITIVITY BY CONGRATULATING THEM ON AN ACHIEVEMENT, TELLING THEM SOMETHING YOU ADMIRE ABOUT THEM, OR GIVING THEM A COMPLIMENT.

THINK ABOUT IT

1 How do the images and messages we are exposed to from the media influence how we see our bodies? Can you think of one way the media promotes a positive body image?

2 Think about what types of social media sites you and your classmates use. How do you think they might influence the way you see yourself?

3 Read the strategies for developing healthy self-esteem and body image on pages 15, 25, and 28. Talk with your peers about strategies that you have tried or would like to try. Can you think of another strategy that you can use to think more highly of yourself and your appearance?

GLOSSARY

able-bodied	Not physically disabled; having a healthy and strong body
blemishes	Small marks or flaws
consumers	People who buy goods and services
conventionally attractive	An appearance that is viewed by the majority of people as being beautiful
corporations	A company or group of people with authority
discriminated	Treated unfairly based on arbitrary reasons, such as race, gender, or age
distorted	Misrepresented or out-of-shape with reality
diversity	The state of being diverse or having variety
eating disorders	Mental health conditions in which a person has abnormal eating habits or experiences extreme stress related to food and eating
edited	To have changed something
endorphins	Chemicals in the body that can help reduce pain and help us feel relaxed
engage	To participate or become involved in
gender	Different from sex; the state of being male or female in relation to social constructs
idealized	Represented as better than reality
identity	A person's view of who they are
mass communication	Reaching large groups of people
mental health	Relating to a person's emotional well-being
minority	A smaller group in relation to a larger one
misinform	To give false or inaccurate information
misrepresentation	Deliberately presenting something falsely or in a misleading way
multicultural	A society that includes several different cultural or ethnic groups
perceptions	Ways of seeing things
permanent	Lasting forever
qualities	Traits or characteristics
reinforce	To support or strengthen an idea
responsibility	Being accountable or obliged to do something
self-worth	One's perception of their importance and abilities
sex appeal	Being attractive in a sexual way
stylists	People whose job it is to arrange and coordinate clothes
temporary	Only lasting for a short time
unique	Being the only one of its kind
value	Consider something to be important
whitewash	The featuring of fair skin and European features as being the most beautiful, and the overrepresentation of white actors in the media or the casting of white actors in roles meant for nonwhite characters

INDEX